**W9-AZG-403**

ANCIENT CULTURES AND CIVILIZATIONS

# THE CULTURE OF
# ATHENS

## Vic Kovacs

# PowerKiDS
press.™

NEW YORK

Published in 2017 by **The Rosen Publishing Group, Inc.**
29 East 21st Street, New York, NY 10010

Cataloging-in-Publication Data

Names: Kovacs, Vic.
Title: The culture of Athens / Vic Kovacs.
Description: New York : PowerKids Press, 2017. | Series: Ancient cultures and civilizations | Includes index.
Identifiers: ISBN 9781508150046 (pbk.) | ISBN 9781508150008 (library bound) | ISBN 9781508149903 (6 pack)
Subjects: LCSH: Greece--Civilization--To 146 B.C.--Juvenile literature. | Athens (Greece)--Social life
    and customs--Juvenile literature.Athens (Greece)--Civilization--Juvenile literature.
Classification: LCC DF77.K68 2017 | DDC 938'.5--d23

Developed and produced for Rosen by BlueAppleWorks Inc.

Art Director: Haley Harasymiw
Managing Editor for BlueAppleWorks: Melissa McClellan
Editors: Janice Dyer, Marcia Abramson
Design: T.J. Choleva

Picture credits: p. 7 www.ohiochannel.org/Creative Commons; p. 9 Philipp Foltz/Public Domain; p. 9 right
Adam Carr/Creative Commons; p. 11 Marie-Lan Nguyen/Creative Commons; p. 12 Metro-Goldwyn-Mayer/
Photofest Copyright_notice: ©Metro-Goldwyn-Mayer Photographer: Eric Carpenter; p. 17, 29 Anastasios71/
Shutterstock; p. 17 inset Samot/Shutterstock; p. 18 left Jastrow/Public Domain; p. 18 Leo von Klenze/Public
Domain; p. 19 inset Haris vythoulkas/Shutterstock; p. 19 elgreko/Shutterstock; p. 20 Marsyas/Creative
Commons; p. 22 Public Domain; p. 24 Carole Raddato/Creative Commons; p. 27 lornet/Shutterstock;
p. 28 Niradj/Shutterstock; Map Illustrations: p. 5 T.J. Choleva/Shutterstock: AridOcean; p. 14 T.J. Choleva/
Shutterstock: Alfonso de Tomas

Manufactured in the United States of America
CPSIA Compliance Information: Batch #BS16PK: For Further Information contact Rosen Publishing, New York, New York at 1-800-237-9932

# CONTENTS

# CHAPTER 1

# ANCIENT ATHENS

Athens was one of the largest and most important **city-states** in all of ancient **Greece**. It is located near the middle of the country. With its famous **Acropolis** at its center, Athens's geographic features contributed to its growth and success. One of the most important features was its closeness to the Sarconic Gulf, a body of water that is part of the Aegean Sea. This closeness led to Athens becoming a major port for trade, and allowed it to become a major naval power.

Humans have lived in Athens for about 5,000 years. The city's first settlers, the Mycenaean people, managed to avoid an invasion from Dorians in about 1200 B.C. The Dorians went on to conquer and settle much of the Peloponnesian region to the south, including **Sparta**. This would lead to a difference in culture between the two cities for generations. By the mid-fifth century B.C., Athens was a center of law, philosophy, art, architecture, and medicine, and had the strongest navy in Greece. Athens is often called the "birthplace of **democracy**." Many of the ideas that form the core of civilization today were created there.

Athens was one of the most powerful cities in ancient Greece. It controlled a region called Attica, a peninsula in the Aegean Sea.

Aegean Sea

ATTICA

Athens

Sarconic Gulf

Peloponnese Peninsula

Crete

# CHAPTER 2

# BIRTH OF DEMOCRACY

From the eighth century B.C. to the sixth century B.C. Athens was ruled by various **aristocratic** families. These families chose political leaders, or archons, who ensured their interests were looked after. This gave them political control over smaller, poorer families. They also owned most of the land. As a result, the poorer people would often go into **debt** to the aristocrats. If they did not pay back these loans, the less fortunate could be forced into slavery.

To prevent the poorer classes of Athens from rising up in rebellion, an archon named Solon canceled all debts in 594 B.C. He also freed Athenians who had become slaves as a result of them, and made it illegal to make an Athenian citizen a slave. Though Solon helped to establish certain rules that led to democracy, the system of government wouldn't truly begin to take shape until the end of the sixth century B.C. In about 508 B.C., a nobleman named Cleisthenes began a series of reforms. He established ten new tribes made up of different areas from all over Attica, the area including and surrounding Athens. As a result, previous partnerships were eliminated. It became hard for one particular place to become powerful, since tribe members were from different geographic areas. It also gave all Athenian citizens an equal voice in politics, regardless of wealth. This equality was the true start of democracy.

Cleisthenes was a nobleman from Athens. He is often called "the father of Athenian democracy."

# THE ECCLESIA

Athenian democracy was made up of three different bodies. The Ecclesia, also called the assembly, was the central one. It was a large meeting that any adult Athenian male citizen could attend. Meetings were held on a hill called the Pnyx. Usually about 5,000 citizens were present. At these meetings, matters of public importance were presented to citizens. It was here that declarations were announced, like entering a war. New laws were also outlined, with positions for and against being argued. Elections for public office took place in the Ecclesia, and at first, trials related to political matters took place there. When it came time to vote, members of the assembly simply raised their hands, with the majority winning.

# THE BOULE

The second institution of Athenian democracy was the Boule. This was a council of five hundred men. The members weren't elected by the population, but drew lots, like a lottery. Leaving the selection of the council completely to chance was considered the fairest method. Each of the ten tribes of Athens contributed fifty members, all over the age of thirty.

The main responsibility of the Boule was to prepare the matters that were to be brought before the assembly. So, everything discussed at the Ecclesia was chosen by

## DO OR DIE

The Ecclesia reviewed the behavior of elected officials before they held office and while they were in office. The assembly could also remove any official from office at any time. If officials did not perform adequately, they could be given the death penalty.

The Ecclesia gathered on the Pnyx for their meetings. The hill was one of the most important places in the creation of democracy. Tourists still visit it today.

and decided on by the Boule. It also handled many of the administrative tasks that went into running Athens.

## THE DIKASTERIA

The third body was the Dikasteria, the courts of ancient Athens. As in the Boule, the juries that decided the cases were chosen randomly. Cases were brought before the court by individuals, who were expected to make their own arguments. In cases against private individuals, the jury was normally made up of two hundred people, while in matters of public institutions they had as many as five hundred members. As in the assembly, guilt or innocence was decided by majority. The jury's decision was absolute.

# CHAPTER 3

# MILITARY MIGHT OF ATHENS

The Athenian **military** was made up of two main groups: the army and the **navy**. The army, composed mostly of foot soldiers called **hoplites**, fought ground battles. The navy, made up of Athens' impressive fleet of ships, fought battles on the sea. Though their army wasn't as feared or as capable as that of Sparta, their rivals to the south, Athens's navy was the largest and most powerful in Greece.

## HOPLITES

In Athens, there was no professional military. At the age of eighteen, every male citizen had two years of military training. After the training was completed, they were eligible to be called up for active duty until the age of sixty. When not actively serving, they worked at other jobs, such as farming. The wealthier of these citizens tended to become hoplites in the army.

Hoplites were armored foot soldiers that formed the main body of the **infantry** in most ancient Greek armies. Hoplites were usually from the upper classes of Athenian society because they were expected to

## NAMED AFTER THEIR SHIELDS

The word hoplite comes from *hoplon*, which was the ancient Greek word for the type of shield they carried.

Ancient Greek pottery often shows military scenes with hoplites. Museums around the world have examples of this pottery.

buy their own armor, which was expensive. As a result, every hoplite was outfitted differently, and there was no standard uniform. Most hoplites had at least a bronze helmet, sometimes with a faceplate, a shield, a long spear, and a smaller sword. They also wore hand and leg armor. Those who could afford it wore bronze breastplates, while those who could not wore a tunic of layered **linen**. Because of its cost, armor was often passed down through generations. Individual pieces of armor were replaced as needed.

## THE NAVY

While the army was home to the wealthier citizens of Athens, the navy was the domain of the poorer, working class citizens. After all, there was no need to buy fancy armor to pull an oar.

Thousands of people on shore often watched naval battles raging at sea. These battles were much more of a spectacle than the hoplite battles on land were.

## THE NAVY AS DEMOCRACY

Many viewed the navy as an important symbol of Athens. It was the source of much of Athens' military and financial power, but it was also more than that. Many different oarsmen, from different backgrounds, worked together for a single purpose. For some, this symbolized the democracy of Athens, with all citizens coming together to decide the city's **destiny**.

The Athenian navy's main weapon was the trireme, a ship with three rows of oars. Each oar was pulled by a single man, and each ship carried 170 rowers. At its height, Athens had a fleet of two hundred of these ships, the largest in Greece. Each trireme was equipped with a heavy bronze battering ram on its front. This was the ship's main method of attack. With every oarsman rowing at full strength, it was able to easily sink enemy ships.

The navy wasn't just interested in matters of war. It also explored and conquered new regions. The navy helped in trade with other cities and nations, which only increased Athens's wealth.

## THE DELIAN LEAGUE

Beginning in 499 B.C., most of Greece was united against a common enemy, the **Persian Empire**. This **alliance**, led by the military superpower Sparta, successfully fought back repeated invasion attempts. By 478 B.C., the Persians had been repelled from mainland Greece. Sparta and its allies considered this the end of hostilities.

Athens, however, believed it needed to safeguard Greek settlements in Asia. Athens also sought revenge on Persia for its actions during the war, including burning down the evacuated Athens.

In an attempt to recruit allies to take the fight to the Persians, a new alliance was formed, called the Delian League. Athens was chosen as the leader of the Delian League because of its powerful navy. Members gained entry to the League in one of two ways: they could send forces from their own militaries, or they could contribute a tax. Paying the tax was the more popular option.

The war between the Greek Delian League and Persians was called the Greco-Persian War. As the war continued, the Delian League began to serve Athens's interests more and more.

The Delian League was named for the island of Delos, where its first meeting was held.

Black Sea

Adriatic Sea    Ancient Greece

Italy

Persian Empire

Aegean Sea

**The Delian League**
- Delos Island    ○ Athens
- ■ Athenian Territory    ○ Marathon Plain
- ■ Territory of Allied City-States

## THE BATTLE OF MARATHON

One of the most important battles of the Greco-Persian War was the Battle of Marathon. Fought in 490 B.C., it took place on the Marathon plain northeast of Athens, in Attica. The Greeks numbered about 10,000 hoplites, while the Persians, according to some reports, had double that number of men. The general Miltiades lined up his forces and ordered them to attack. Meeting the Persians, the center of the Greek army broke, but its left and right **flanks** held strong. The flanks managed to surround the Persians, who were massacred. In the end, 6,400 Persians were killed, while the Greeks counted just 192 dead. The legend says that a messenger ran 26 miles (42 kilometers) back to Athens and dropped dead after delivering the news of victory. It's claimed that this is where the modern marathon run comes from.

As the leading city-state in the league, Athens began to exert stricter control over their allies, as well as conquering and colonizing other regions. By 454 B.C., the Delian League was less of an alliance and more of an Athenian empire.

During this time, Athens began several construction projects. One of these was building the Long Walls that connected Athens to Piraeus, the city where its port was located. These walls helped to make it almost impossible to attack from land. This, along with Athens's increasingly arrogant attitude, lead to tensions, especially with Sparta. Peace was finally achieved with Persia in 450 B.C. By that time, however, the stage was already set for a conflict between Athens and Sparta, Greece's two main powers. The conflict would come to be known as the Peloponnesian War.

# CHAPTER 4

# LIFE IN ATHENS

During its height, Athens was one of the most advanced cultures in the world. Its contributions to many different fields, such as architecture, philosophy, and medicine, are still relevant today. In fact, as well as being the "birthplace of democracy," Athens is often considered to be the birthplace of these important domains!

## ARCHITECTURE

There were three main styles of Greek architecture: Doric, Ionic, and Corinthian. Each of these styles was recognizable by the types of columns it used. The simplest of these, and the most popular in Athens, was the Doric style. Doric columns were widest in the middle, and slightly thinner at the top. They had twenty vertical grooves carved into them, called flutes. The capital, a stone circle, was placed on top of the column. On top of the capital was a square stone called the abacus. These columns held up the **entablature**, which was often decorated with carvings of people or other figures in spaces called metopes.

The most famous example of Athenian architecture is the Parthenon. Built between 447 and 438 B.C., it was constructed as a temple to the goddess Athena. It was made of white marble, and given a place of honor on the Acropolis.

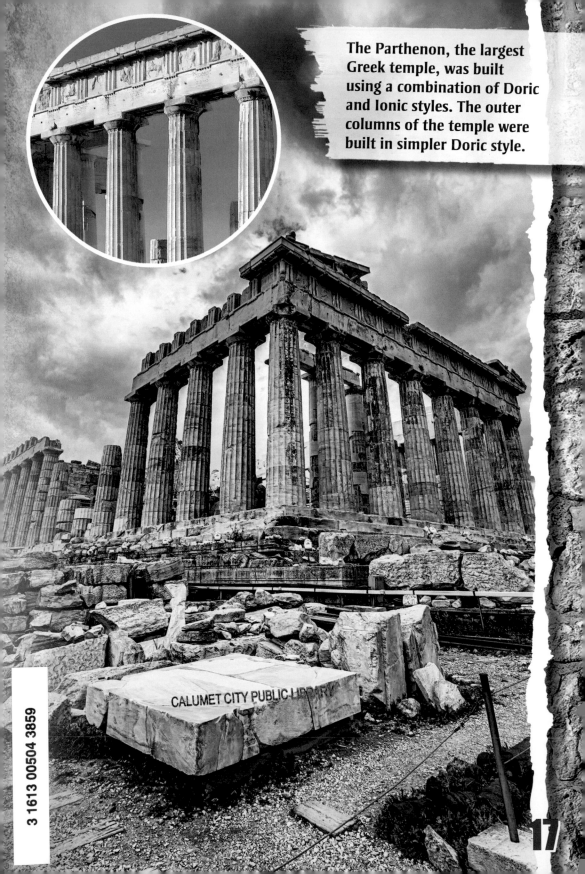

The Parthenon, the largest Greek temple, was built using a combination of Doric and Ionic styles. The outer columns of the temple were built in simpler Doric style.

The sculptures in the metopes depicted battles between god and man, centaurs, and other scenes that have been lost to time. The fact that it still stands today is a testament to the strength of Greek architecture. The Parthenon is considered the height of the Doric style.

## RELIGION AND WORSHIP

Athenians, like most ancient Greeks, worshipped the Twelve Olympians. These twelve gods were masters of different domains, and as a result, different gods would be prayed to, depending on what was being asked for. For example, a general might pray to Ares, the god of war, to help his army win an important battle. Athena, the goddess of wisdom, was particularly important to Athenians, as the city was named after her.

The Parthenon was a sacred building dedicated to the goddess Athena. In ancient Greece, Athena was the goddess of wisdom, courage, justice, arts, and literature.

The Temple of Zeus was built between 472 and 456 B.C. It was dedicated to Zeus, king of the Olympian gods. The temple was built in more decorative Corinthian style.

Temples were often the most amazing architectural achievements in ancient Greece, and Athens was no exception. In ancient Greece, worship took place outside of temples. Inside was usually just a room with a statue of the god the temple was dedicated to. Worshippers would generally only enter to leave offerings directly to this statue.

Athenians held many festivals each year to honor their gods. The most important of these was the Panathenaea, which celebrated Athena's birthday. It involved a large procession that made its way through the Acropolis. Other festivals involved feasts, plays, and competitions.

## FAMILY LIFE

Growing up in Athens was very different for boys and girls. All children stayed with their families until they were seven years old, but after that, they began down different paths.

At the age of seven, boys began attending school. There they were taught a variety of subjects to prepare them for their lives as citizens. At the age of eighteen, all boys began two years of military training. Men were expected to work to support their household and pay taxes to the state. Only male citizens were allowed to vote.

Women in ancient Athens had few choices. They could not vote or own property. Their life was focused on running the household and raising children.

Women spent most of their time in a part of the house called the gynaeceum. This area was far away from the areas in the house for men and from the street.

## THE LEGEND OF ATHENS' NAME

An ancient Athenian legend says that when the city was created, it was originally called Ceropia, after its founder. However, the gods were so impressed by the city that each of them wished to become its patron, and have the city named after them. The two fiercest competitors for this honor were Poseidon, god of the sea, and Athena, goddess of wisdom. To resolve the matter, Zeus, king of the gods, told the two to give a gift to the new city. The citizens would choose the gift they preferred, and its giver would be the victor. Poseidon created a stream, which implied that the city would enjoy naval supremacy. Athena dropped a seed that instantly grew into an olive tree. The citizens, recognizing that Athena was offering them peace and prosperity, chose her gift.

Girls did not attend school, but instead stayed home with their mothers. This helped to prepare them for their roles as wives and mothers. Athenian girls usually married around the age of fourteen, and were expected to run the household. They rarely left the house, and did not hold jobs.

Most households had at least one slave. They were property of their masters, who could do whatever they wanted with them. Compared to other Greek states, Athenian slaves were relatively well treated. Much of the manual labor in a household, and in the city in general, fell to slaves. Occasionally, slaves were able to save up enough money to buy their freedom.

# EDUCATION, ARTS AND CULTURE

Athens was the center for education and culture in ancient Greece. Only boys attended school, and all the teachers were male. Tuition costs were low, so even the poorest Athenians could afford to send their children to school for at least a few years. The goal of education was to train citizens in the arts and to prepare them for peace and war. Basic education started at age six and ended at age sixteen. At the age of eighteen, students began two years of military training.

The students took three main courses: grammata, music, and physical education. Grammata included reading, writing, and arithmetic. Students studied the famous poets, such as Homer, and explored the **feats** of Greek heroes.

During the golden age of Athens, great thinkers and many writers and artists from all corners of Greece lived and worked in the city.

## ATHENIAN PHILOSOPHERS

Ancient Athens contributed many things to the world, but one of the most important was its innovations in the way people thought. The three great Athenian philosophers, Socrates, Plato, and Aristotle, asked questions that had never before been considered. They are still studied today, and a clear line can be drawn from them to modern philosophy. The Socratic method, described by Plato, formed the basis for much of philosophy, and also the scientific method.

Music included singing, playing instruments such as the lyre and the flute, reciting, and performing poetry musically. Physical education included wrestling, jumping, running, and throwing discus and javelin. It helped students become fit and healthy citizens.

Girls received a different kind of schooling. They remained at home and learned the skills that were needed to run a household. Their mothers or a private tutor sometimes taught girls to read and write, and to play an instrument. Girls also took part in sports, such as wrestling. This instruction continued until the girl married and left home.

Athens was also famous as a city rich in art and culture. Some of the greatest artists in history have been inspired by surviving examples of Athenian sculpture. Children were taught to sing the epic poems of Homer in schools, and the festival Dionysia brought large groups together to watch plays by popular writers of the day.

## SPORTS AND ATHLETES

Athletics were popular in all of Greece. In Athens, it was believed that a healthy body would help develop a healthy mind. This was important to Athenians, as one needed to be clearheaded to vote on matters that would affect the whole city. The Panathenaea, Athens' most important festival, involved athletic competitions.

The city was an active competitor in the Panhellenic Games. These were four regular festivals that involved very similar sporting events. The festivals were held in a four-year cycle. The first, and most important, were the Olympic Games. The following year, the Nemian and Isthmian games were held in different months. The year after that was the Pythian Games, and in the fourth year of the cycle the Nemian and Isthmian games repeated. Then the whole cycle started over again with the Olympics.

**Victors at the Olympics were celebrated and honored. The stories of their feats were told for future generations.**

## THE OLYMPIC GAMES

Though the ancient Olympics were very different from the events held today, they did have some things in common. They happened every four years, just like today, and they involved various athletic competitions. However, instead of changing locations, they always happened at Olympia, in the Peloponnese region of the country. They also had a religious side, as they were held to honor Zeus, the king of the gods.

Events were only open to Greek men. They included contests of strength, such as boxing and wrestling. There were also chariot races, and events that would be considered track and field today, such as the discus toss and long jump. The most popular events were the footraces. The hoplitodromos, the final footrace of the games, was run wearing 50 pounds (23 kg) of armor!

Like most Greek festivals, these competitions were not only about sports. They also had an artistic side, as well as a religious aspect. The ancient Athenians tried to balance development of the body, mind, and soul. As a result, music, drama, poetry, and visual arts contests were held along with athletic competitions. Each festival was held in honor of a different god. They also helped unite the country. A **truce** took effect during the games, and whatever fighting was going on between city-states at the time was halted. People would flock to the games from all corners of Greece and its colonies, both to participate and to watch. The physical prize wasn't terribly impressive. It was just a wreath. The real prize, though, was the glory and the honor that would be gained with victory. Having a champion of the games from your city was a major source of pride.

# CHAPTER 5

# DOWNFALL AND LEGACY

The Peloponnesian War, fought between Athens and Sparta, lasted for almost thirty years, beginning in 431 B.C. There was a period of truce from 421 to 414 B.C., when fighting began again. Almost as soon as the war broke out, Athens was devastated by a **plague**. It killed almost a third of the city's population, including its leader, Pericles. The loss of much of their fighting force to illness, as well as their leader, was not a good sign for the Athenian war effort. Modern scholars are still unsure exactly which disease the plague actually was. What isn't in dispute, though, is that it was the beginning of the end of Athens's golden period.

The war finally ended for good, with Athens's defeat, in 404 B.C. For most of the war, the two city-states seemed to be at a **stalemate**. Athens's navy was far superior to that of Sparta, but their army was generally outclassed by the professional soldiers of Sparta. Near the war's end, Sparta went to their old enemies, the Persian Empire, and received money to fund a navy. They were able to finally break Athens.

After their defeat, the city was banned from having a navy, its great walls were torn down, and it entered a period of decline. Athens never again reached the heights of power and influence it knew as the leader of the Delian League.

Philosopher Plato founded the first university in the Western world in Athens near a sacred grove of olive trees dedicated to Athena.

By 146 B.C., Athens, along with the rest of Greece, became members of the **Roman Empire**, following the destruction of the city of Corinth. Today, Athens is a modern city, the largest in Greece, as well as its capital. Over three million people live there, and they enjoy a democracy first dreamed up by their ancestors over two thousand years ago. Though it is a modern city, it has ancient buildings still standing, including the Parthenon, alongside works of art that are thousands of years old.

Though it is no longer an independent city-state, the many innovations made by Athens during its golden period continue to affect the world today. Its experiment with democracy led to the free governments that many countries now enjoy. When the founding fathers of the United States were discussing what form of government their new country should use, they were inspired by the ancient Athenians.

Governments in Greece and Europe are working together to protect and conserve the famous buildings in Athens, such as the Parthenon on the Acropolis.

Modern Athens is an important city because of its location and its economy. The port Piraeus is the second-largest passenger port in the world.

Surviving sculptures from ancient Athens continue to inspire artists throughout the ages. The city's great thinkers and philosophers created the building blocks of modern thinking, and their ideas are still taught in universities everywhere. A version of the Olympic Games created by the Athenians still exists today. However, instead of just uniting Greece, the modern games unite the whole world in friendly competition. Perhaps never before has a city so incredibly affected the world around us. Its influence is still felt today, and will continue to be felt in the future.

## BACK IN THE GAME

Modern Athens hosted the first modern Olympic Games in 1896! The city hosted them again most recently in 2004.

# GLOSSARY

**acropolis:** the upper, fortified part of a city, particularly a city in ancient Greece such as Athens

**alliance:** a formal agreement between two or more people, regions, or nations

**aristocratic:** a member of the ruling class

**city-state:** a city that also has other areas outside of itself that depend on it

**debt:** something owed, such as money

**democracy:** a form of government where people choose leaders by voting

**destiny:** one's fate

**entablature:** the upper section of a building that rests on the columns

**feat:** an act of skill, strength, or endurance

**flank:** the right or left side of an army

**Greece:** a country in the southeast part of Europe

**hoplite:** a foot soldier in ancient Greece

**infantry:** foot soldiers, soldiers who fight on the ground

**linen:** a type of woven cloth

**military:** an organized group of soldiers who protect and fight for the interests of a city, state, or country

**navy:** a part of the military concerned with battles on the sea and ocean

**peninsula:** a piece of land with water on three sides, but that is still connected to a larger land mass

**Persian Empire:** an ancient dynasty based in what is today known as Iran

**plague:** a very infectious, usually fatal, disease

**Roman Empire:** the territories ruled by ancient Rome, the city based in a region that today is known as Italy

**Sparta:** a city-state in the south of Greece, famous for its military focused society

**stalemate:** a deadlock

**truce:** a temporary end of fighting

# FOR MORE INFORMATION

## Books

Caper, William. *Ancient Greece: An Interactive History Adventure* North Mankato, MN: Capstone Press, 2010.

Leavitt, Amie Jane. *Ancient Athens*. Newark, DE: Mitchell Lane Publishers, Inc., 2012.

Newman, Sandra. *Ancient Greece*. New York: Scholastic, 2010.

Pearson, Anne. *Ancient Greece*. New York: DK Eyewitness Books, 2014.

## Websites

Due to the changing nature of Internet links, PowerKids Press has developed an online list of websites related to the subject of this book. This site is updated regularly. Please use this link to access the list:

**www.powerkidslinks.com/acc/athens**

# INDEX